What reader

Still-life of a

"Heart-rending. A lesson to all those people who don't take this seriously. It should be read by everyone."
Astrid Kerby (South Africa)

"Brilliant. So accurate to how we're feeling. Blown away !"
Heidi Flax (South Africa)

"This poem reflects with articulate and painful empathy what so many families have been through."
Rabbi Jonathan Wittenberg (UK)

"I'm not one for reading poetry, but I've been reading some since this lockdown. Although *Broll's* verse appears simple, that brevity belies a rich intensity of emotion beneath. It makes the poem approachable and easy to read, it has a lot to say, but also rewards reading over and over. Simple phrases have surprising layers of meaning, which is skilful.
I'm glad I read it and it has encouraged me
to read more !"
Doctor Gary Evans (UK)

Still-life
of a
Pandemic

by
Brandon Broll

COPYRIGHT

Published by Riols Quarter Ltd.
85 Great Portland Street, London W1W 7LT.
Company registered in England and Wales.
Company number: 12673832

ISBN 978-1-913758-01-1

Cover design by More Visual Ltd.
Illustrations by Barbara Jackson

CONTENTS

A poem in five parts

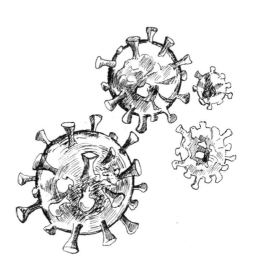

they say that the dead are walking
in the minds of the people talking
the fear of this virus stalking
in the street of the hollow eyes

it's still, a still-life
a life of stillness
yet still you are alive
yet still you are alive

officials speak their daily briefing
the death count without weeping
social distance is impairing
in the street of the hollow eyes

still it's a still-life
stillness of a life
you are alive still
yet still you are alive

all eyes upon the sneeze
it's hay fever in the breeze
cup your mouth if you please
in the street of the hollow eyes

thank heavens she didn't cough
the mask tight over her mouth
the deadly fear of going south
in the street of the hollow eyes

it's still, a still-life
a life of stillness
yet still you are alive
yet still you are alive

kids lie on beds unmade
do their homework ungraded
yawn their boredom unsaid
in the street of the hollow eyes

still it's a still-life
stillness of a life
you are alive still
yet still you are alive

parents queue in equal spaces
food shop or chemist places
the shared glances of neighbourhood faces
in the street of the hollow eyes

wash your hands every time
you return, don't think I'm blind
covid-19 is such a grind
in the street of the hollow eyes

it's still, a still-life
a life of stillness
yet still you are alive
yet still you are alive

the fever comes by chance
I isolate fast
the wife's worried glance
in the street of the hollow eyes

still it's a still-life
stillness of a life
you are alive still
yet still you are alive

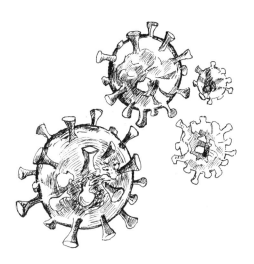

2

the cough comes later
my lungs in a grater
try not to be a hater
in the street of the hollow eyes

when the gasping arrives
in the street of the hollow eyes
they take me away
eyes liquid, face pale grey

it's still, a still-life
a life of stillness
yet still you are alive
yet still you are alive

masked man above my face
in this small ambulance space
I close my eyes, cannot linger
pulse oximeter on my finger

he straps a mask over my chin
says to breathe the oxygen in
delirium dissolves as my friend
in and out, end to end

still it's a still-life
stillness of a life
you are alive still
yet still you are alive

hospital lights are ever bright
"he's contesting a good fight !"
I hear a doctor say
in my distant haze of delay

but he's going downhill fast
a whisper that I hear at last
his basal breathing is fraught
it's worse than we thought

it's still, a still-life
a life of stillness
yet still you are alive
yet still you are alive

all my body is aching
it feels completely overtaken
needles prick into my skin
toxic virus exploding within

this gowned medical army
on the one side alarms me
unseen *covid* on the other
help me, help me, mother !

still it's a still-life
stillness of a life
you are alive still
yet still you are alive

"darling, we love you !"
voices emerge out of the blue
I hear my wife weeping
my older son is speaking

masked nurse presses the phone
to my ear, they hear me groan
before the blissful sedation
the unconscious elation

it's still, a still-life
a life of stillness
yet still you are alive
yet still you are alive

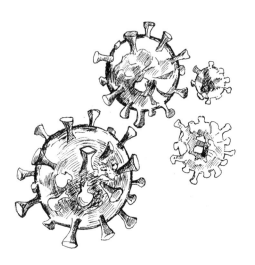

at home the panicked wife
contemplates her tenuous life
trembling hand with a knife
in the street of the hollow eyes

she cannot stomach any food
cooks for her sons in subdued mood
fear exposed in her eyes
what happens if her love dies ?

still it's a still-life
stillness of a life
you are alive still
yet still you are alive

her sons help to occupy her mind
with activities which they find
youth assists you to be blind
in the street of the hollow eyes

they walk thoughtfully in their local park
practice avoidance with a smile
every person is a viral spark
keep your distance all the while

it's still, a still-life
a life of stillness
yet still you are alive
yet still you are alive

at night she turns and dreams of him
sweating, coughing, then the medics came
her sobs are pillow muffled and grim
in the street of the hollow eyes

each dawn she phones the ward
"intensive care, hello, can I help ?"
have you news of how he is ?
we're his family waiting, please !

still it's a still-life
stillness of a life
you are alive still
yet still you are alive

no matter she intercepts the early shift
nursing kindness behind muffled mask
they cannot give her the glorious lift
in the street of the hollow eyes

she wants her friends, she doesn't
know what she wants incumbent
is losing her mind to the moment
in the street of the hollow eyes

it's still, a still-life
a life of stillness
yet still you are alive
yet still you are alive

her days and nights become leaden
she smiles away the pain to deaden
the fear that her sons are expressing
in the street of the hollow eyes

they huddle and comfort each other
where will this take us dear brother
we will look after you mother
in the street of the hollow eyes

still it's a still-life
stillness of a life
you are alive still
yet still you are alive

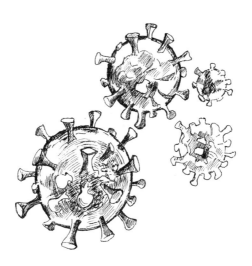

4

I am sinking into morphine
hooded men in gowns of green
"intubate" they agree a plan
chin up, mouth wide, tube in

he won't remember when it's over
if we induce him into a coma
I have become another waiter
a patient on a ventilator

it's still, a still-life
a life of stillness
yet still you are alive
yet still you are alive

the flights of my fleeting mind
busy medics adjusting switches
hearing sound but I am blind
a slack body with muscle twitches

floating above an island haze
the hum of busy background voices
I am superman ablaze
inside my mind, the infinite choices

still it's a still-life
stillness of a life
you are alive still
yet still you are alive

"hello, can you hear me, darling?"
a nurse prods and pinches my skin
the phone held near is abrupt and startling
"can you hear me, let me in !"

the voice is distant and far away
but now I hear the tenor of you
it draws me back to the here today
to the world beyond this flu

it's still, a still-life
a life of stillness
yet still you are alive
yet still you are alive

they twist and turn me onto my front
dialysis of my kidneys shunt
the blood prickled with viral load
to help my organs that have slowed

they call it an inflammation storm
my immune system in overdrive
the medics cluster, then they warn
my wife: "he just may not survive !"

still it's a still-life
stillness of a life
you are alive still
yet still you are alive

at 4 am the monitor alarms
the beeping and the frenzy of arms
I am floating in another place
I see the smile on my wife's face

the jolting, jostling is outside me
"bye bye my love," I hear her say
the moment comes to float free
"I'll see you in another way !"

it's still, a still-life
a life of stillness
yet still you are alive
yet still you are alive

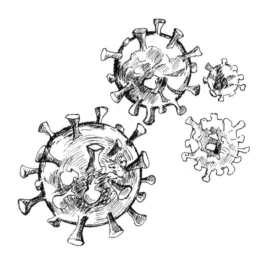

neighbours discover the news fast
their house is marked as people pass
but friends rally, good wishes outlast
in the street of the hollow eyes

still it's a still-life
stillness of a life
you are alive still
yet still you are alive

officials speak their daily briefing
the death count without weeping
it's different if you are grieving
in the street of the hollow eyes

it's still, a still-life
a life of stillness
yet still you are alive
yet still you are alive

unto death you shall be buried
the preparations very hurried
masked men make it scary
in the street of the hollow eyes

body bag in a sealed casket
only five mourners asked
the younger son is video-tasked
in the street of the hollow eyes

still it's a still-life
stillness of a life
you are alive still
yet still you are alive

many people watch on zoom
sitting isolated room to room
unable to visit the family soon
in the street of the hollow eyes

it's still, a still-life
a life of stillness
yet still you are alive
yet still you are alive

bereft, broken, unable to cope
the family of mourners with faltering hope
dedicate a park bench to his name
in the street of the hollow eyes

they sit below a hovering shroud
notice the birdsong especially loud
on this bench, a plaque, they're proud
in the street of the hollow eyes

still it's a still-life
stillness of a life
you are alive still
yet still you are alive

the flowers of spring usher in
the air smells cleansed of pollution
officials announce the lock down easing
in the street of the hollow eyes

it's less of a still-life
less of a life of stillness
yet still you are alive
yet still you are alive

IN MEMORIAM

This poem is dedicated to the enduring memory
of the large number of people
who lost their lives
to *Covid-19*

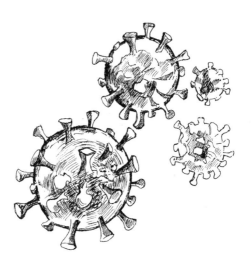

Printed in Great Britain
by Amazon